An Embrace of Dreams

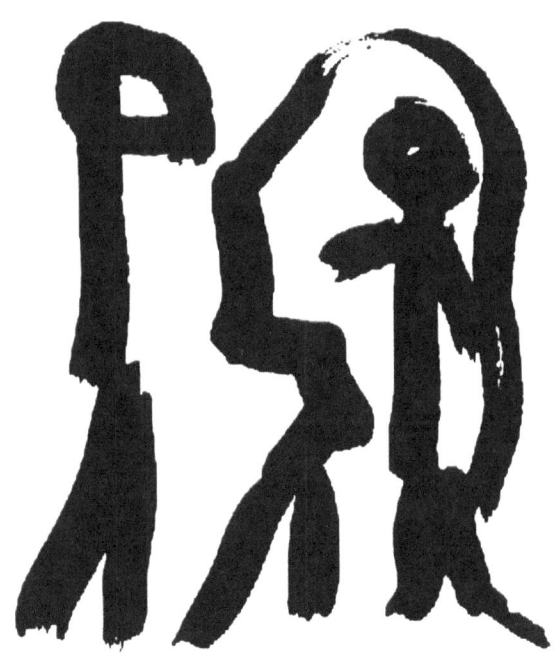

Poems and Ink
from
Varied Times
By
Anthony Marchese

also by Anthony Marchese

Novels

Bobby, Carolina. The Novel

The Dream of Zaragoza Murphy

Books of Poetry

Outfluence: Songs of Quarantine

i hear rustling (English/Spanish)

un attimo fa (italiano)

Symphony of Civilization
    (For the Children of the
      NYC Public School System)

An Embrace of Dreams

Poems and Ink from Varied Times

by

Anthony Marchese

All rights reserved. All characters appearing in this work are fictitious. Any resemblance to real persons, living or dead is purely coincidental. No part of this publication may be reproduced, distributed, or transmitted in any form or by any means, including photocopying, recording, or other electronic or mechanical methods, either now known or unknown, without the written permission of the publisher, except in the case of brief quotations embodied in critical reviews and certain other noncommercial uses permitted by copyright law.

For permission requests, write to the publisher, "Attention: Permissions Coordinator", at the email address below.

outfluence3@gmail.com

© 2024 Anthony Marchese
All Rights Reserved

Versione Augustus 2025

SF Abrazo = Embrace I

Dedicated to my Son.
And all my friends since forever.
Time Does Not Exist.
Here We Are.

I wish you
Peace and Happiness.

after walking across the barren desert they come to a garden of emerald eden. this they thought was the promised land. rivers and streams. trees and plants. rolling grass as far as the eye can see. on the lowest flat they could plant rice and they began to sing.

> "we'll plant maize upon the fairway
> and peppers on the greens
> we will drink the crystal water
> ever flowing in the stream . . ."

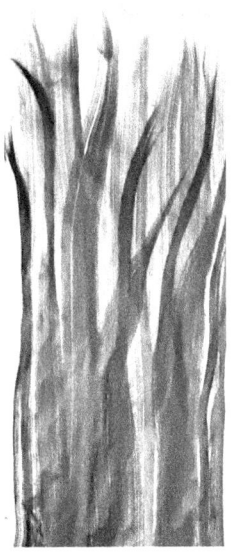

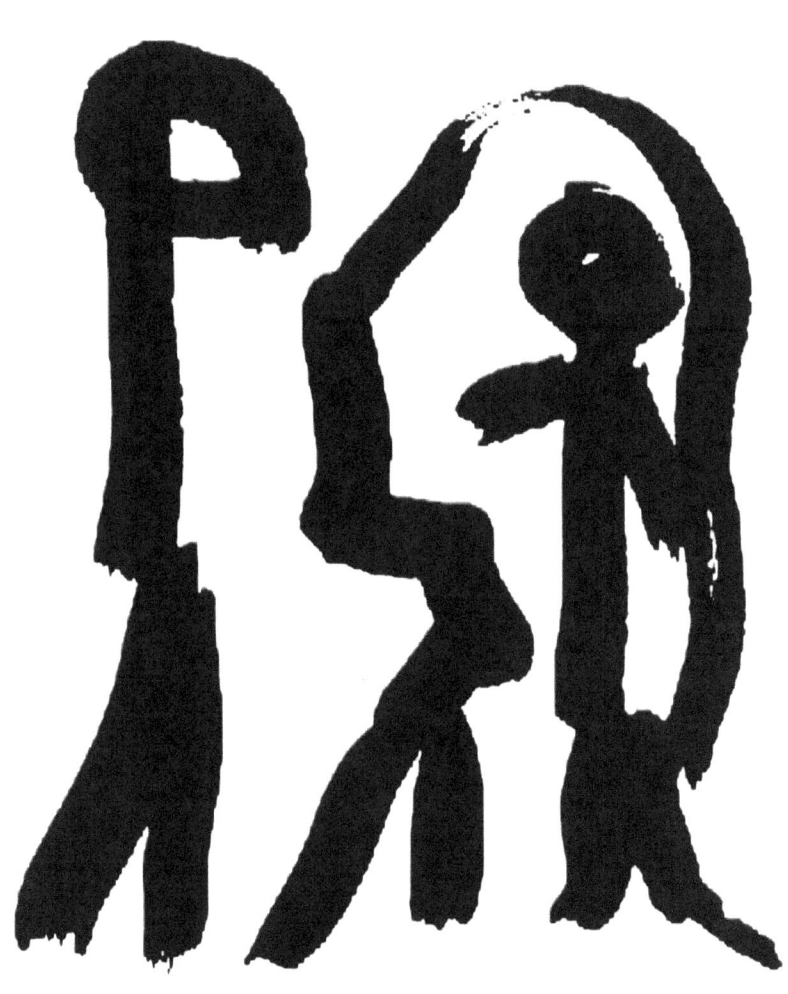

sometimes in the morning
i would wake up
and the writing was written
i do not remember
but i guess it was my fault

no hay culpa
solo verdad

she asks is detroit the same as here?
i answer with all the differences
she says its pretty far huh?
yeah but like i said its pretty much the same

2 feet in a puddle of damp moistened
   dew
2 beats of a heart skipped
               a vision of you

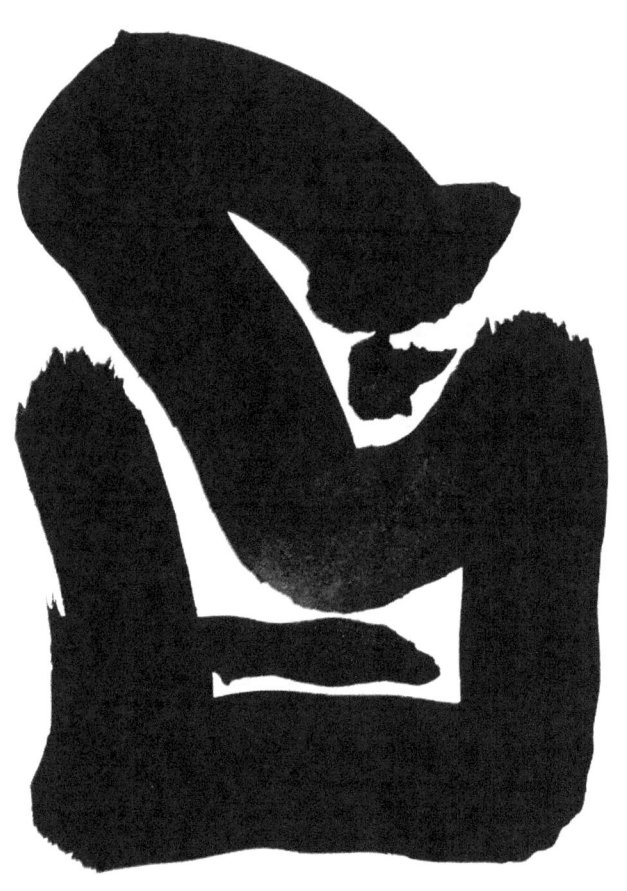

octavio

and the words that i read
say the eight now is dead
thoughts of love and of pain
and the power in his head
raised above the throngs of his people
he wrote verse in a church and
sang from the steeple
that his people were one
not the conqueror and conquered
the people of the sun had made love
with the spaniard
but her crys ring my ears
and your boots choke my tears
as i struggle to plant us the corn
with a stick and a seed
these are all that i need
bubble soil will conquer the worn
over turned over teemed
burnt as offerings in a dream
now our earth is as parched as mother cheeks
if we listen to you
any more we are through
like the time that you taught good is meek
but you cracked and you beat

all of those within your seat
and for that you will sow what you reap
go on your way
in peace i will say
with a smile upon my brown face
this land is our home
not a spoil for your rome
nor the ash of our tome
that was fuel for your roam
dress me in lace
sure to stay in my place
you abuse me though i am your brother
if you read your own words
you would see in each line
that the birds sing
the song of our time
you can not hear the quetzals call
in my grandfathers hall
for the noise of your life
is deafening
nor do you see the true beauty
that surrounds her in piety
what more do you see in me
i curse you on bended knee
silently
i whisper
in the voice of a jaguar
all fours now

slowly moving through the green trees i
hesitate as i sense a foreign presence
towards the foreign presence i slither
a serpent twisting with my shadow twin
and like a lost child i approach the foreigner
obviously lost
could i help you on your way
words i never got a chance to say
because in a moment
not he but my head was whats lost
i did not mean to frighten him

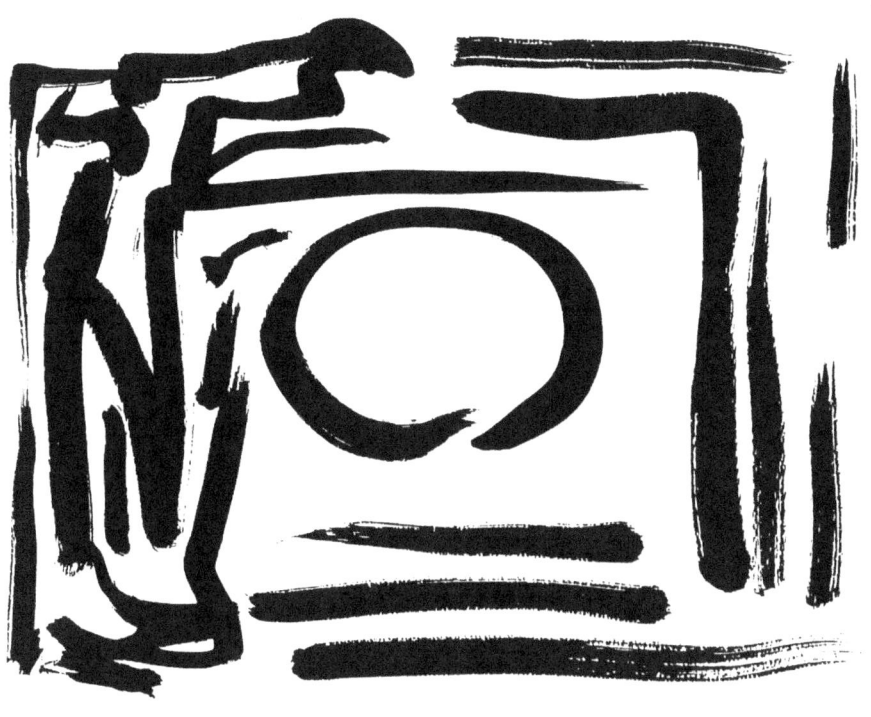

voices from afar drift to pry
sleeping eyes
as drops of rain drip to
blur sleeping eyes
and words within run
in a blur of misty drizzle
cool as the cloud engulfs
    with a moist caress
of morning dew kisses

i love to feel the rain sprinkles
that drift between the pine needles
swirling in the heights
falling from above
for now i sit and watch the
street   buildings   cars
i see the people flee the rain sprinkles

if i took the camera out today
would i put black and white film in it or color
well it is shitty
but remember the rolls are all of 36
i guess we need to do something about that.
although we should be bracketing all of our shots
and remember ing what the numbers were

the reflection dances
on the slick pavement
lights and steel
petroleum

rasta rests in all reflection
cool in the rain pool
laughing
in a dogs other world

is the shadow crawling
across the rains pool
real
or only a reflection of truth

is the truth real
or only a reflection
of the shadow
crawling across the rains pool

rasta laughs at my reflection
sitting over the rain pool
in this human other world

we dance together
across the slick pavement
two shadows of light
stealing a moment s
reflection

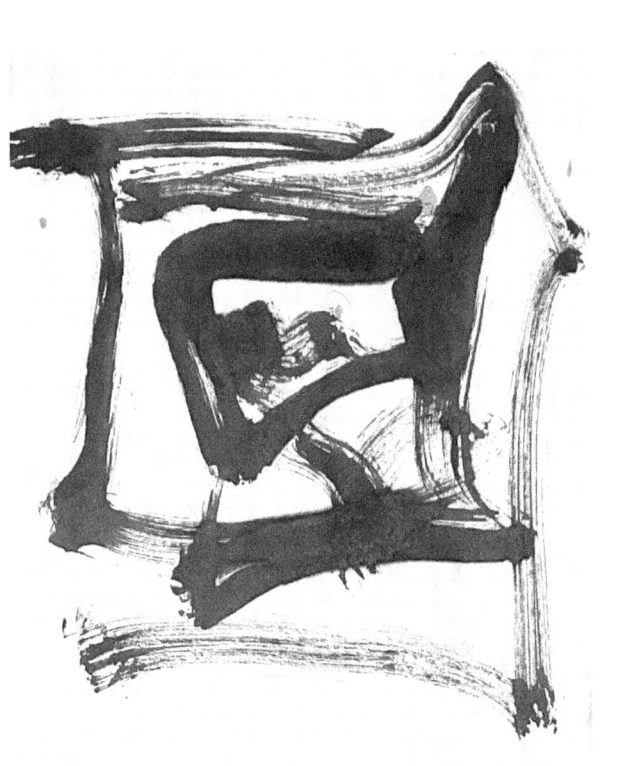

a misty day in the month of may
drifting droplets drizzling sing
and breeze in the palms asway
in windy beauty a morning ring

the Doorstep of the Mind
a friend never arrives at the doorstep of the mind
busy in a dark corner bar drinking times burgundy wine
his true voice shattered in the fireplace of liquor
a potato and a grain in this game always the victor
his eyes in a moment of clarity shout with a knowing glance
his lips are parched and soundless the words dont have a chance
to escape the prison of mindlessness a distant lovers shadow
creeps across his furrowed brow genius in the gallows
shackled to a bitter journey planned far down below
he is born to worship the sun trapped in shadow never known
a sailor born in the mountains never embraces his destinys hand

as a swimmer never sees the sea born of endless land
but in his mind the vision clear if only just a glance
and in a stupor wine did bring his genius has a chance
struggling from within the prison freed by a guardians key
his words will flow and fall from the place that you must see
a phrase slips from the prophet lips now glistening wet with wine
and in a glimpse of flawlessness we reach the doorstep of the mind

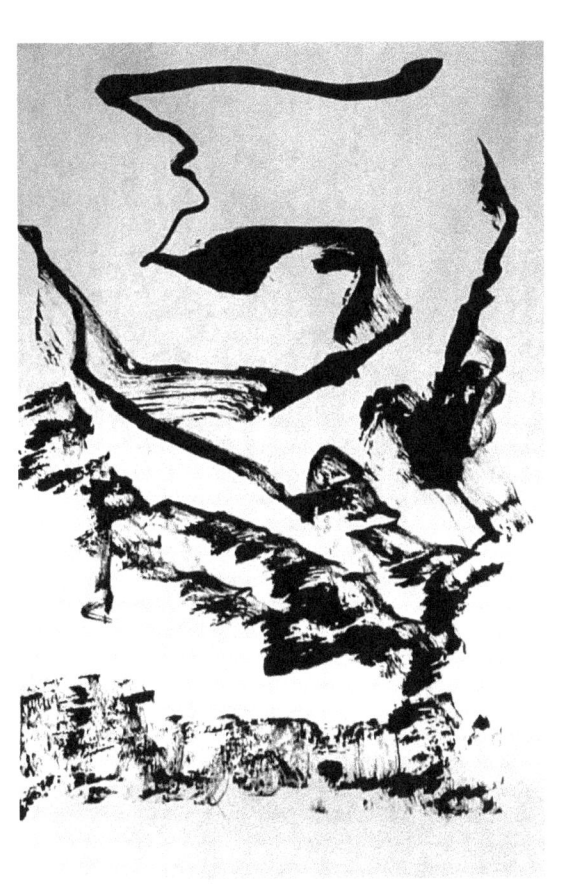

the moon is full in the dark night sky
the sky that hovers above you and i
the bright white glow are the lights in your eye
i see your beauty shine from every star

i see the moon is as bright as a star
i feel her warmth for next to me you are
brighter than the stars on far
because of our closeness and proximity

the moon is where our love will be
i will go there if you will follow me
together our home is where we will be
all you need to do is hold my hand

from the moon we will see the sea and the land
and the peaks and canyon from afar so grand
close to my heart i will hold your hand
here together you and i

together we will see the starry sky
and share the moon that hangs on high
her beams of light will draw a sigh
from the depth of my heart that now is yours

the light of the moon kisses distant shores
passes through the mind locked behind closed doors
to bog down in the exitless moors
a peaceful place to end the day

protected in your embrace where i lay
i will sleep in soft arms that rock and sway
as your hand caresses my fears away
i will dream of the touch of that hand

and run my finger across the sand
on the edge of the sea and the rolling land
the earth as large as the sky is grande
and here on earth are you and i

as we watch above escapes a sigh
for the moon is full in the darkened sky

on wings of words
i fly above
the gentle breeze
is songs of love

the soaring tome
it will glide higher
than the predators dive
into weaknesses fire

and in this shooting hunters form
engulfed and drownd in flaming storm
a cry will rise to clear thoughts heaving
fear in flapping gliding nearing
but fear of love in the gentle breeze
wings of words will vanquish these

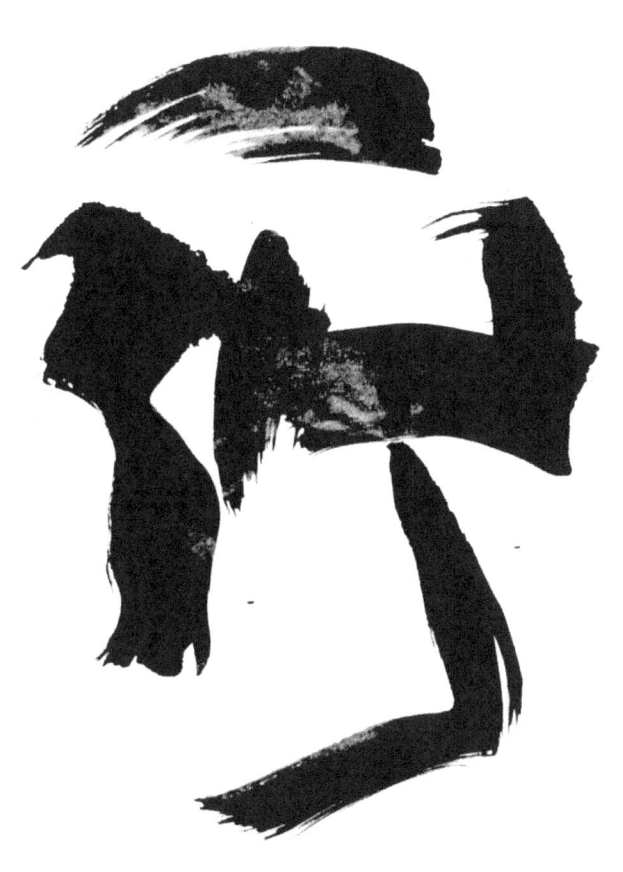

cars drive by outside
rushing in the morning rain
skittering across the black shimmering streets
of a city being taken
taken by time
but truly taken by the takers
the collectors
of citys
entire blocks
buildings
homes
apartments
streets
and sidewalks
gobbled up in the name of democracy
and free markets
dont they realize that the markets do not give
anything away
that is why they must steal in order to have
they buy up all that they see as worth buying up
they destroy what they see that the value is
greater destroyed
and then they build what they see as cost
effective
good profit margin
quality no

quantity as many as we can possibly fit on this
sidewalk
along this street
an apartment
a home
buildings and entire city blocks
destroyed to build the shells of their citys
take away the soul and all that is left is the shell
development out of control
is civilizations road straight to hell
the cars drive by
outside my window
rushing in the morning rain
on a road to nowhere
how do i know
i can hear them

a thought in the heart
as true as the touch of a childs hand
wrapping around an adult finger
the true power is within   and
can not be gauged on the machines of
transitory time
always changing always improving
why this need for continuous change
where does this vacuum originate
why must the emptiness continuously pull the
weak into its vortex
only within can anything be truly measured and
only you can measure the gauge of your truth

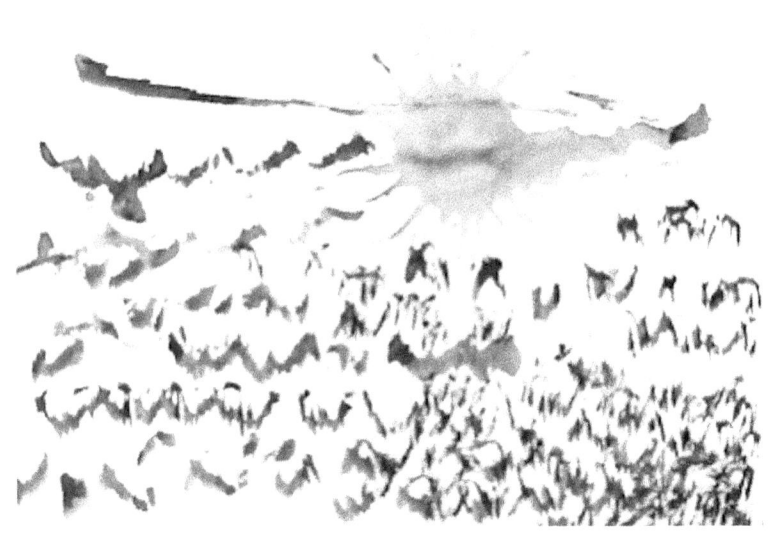

the mexican poet looks out over the sea
to see the caps of a distant shores break
breathe in the salt air
feel the freshness on your skin
the sound of the churning surf
the swirling pools tickling the rocks and sand
the deep blues reaching to embrace the
freshness of the horizons
turquoise
what lies beyond the arc of infinity

the mexican poet looks out over the desert floor
a suharo silhouette kisses the horizon
breathe in the clean air
feel the freshness on your skin
the sound of the tumbling tumbleweed
swirls kicking up in dust the rocks and sand

carpet laid until the clearest touch of azul
shoots from the floor to the ceiling of sky
what lies beyond the jagged horizon

the mexican poet looks out over a mountainous homeland
the horizon held in the hills rocking humps
breathe in the high plains air
feel the crisp cool breeze on your skin
the sound of whistling range
earths movement shifting in a visions blur
the rolling floor the hearth holding
climbing up the foothills of time
what lies beyond this mountainous homeland

the mexican poet hangs above the jungle floor
the nonexistent horizon hiding behind the wall of green
breath in a drink of air
feel the wet heat embrace your skin
surrounding sounds of endless voices
breeze caught in a leaf wall
emerald walls climbing curves to seal the trees ceiling
vines entwined in lacondon time
what lies behind times shadowous jade

i hear church bells ringing
in the city
they seem to arrive from afar
not this city
but a faraway
pueblo
calling to me
to write
to see
to fly
i hear church bells ringing
the call of the chains to the slaves
but now
so far away the sound
of the church bells
is music to my ears

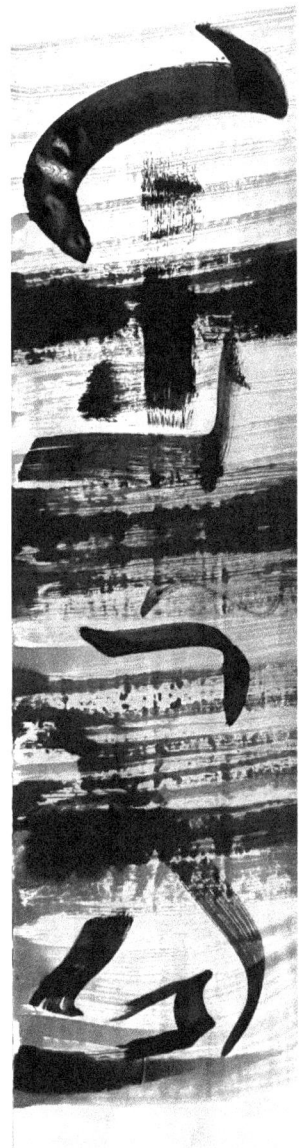

we are who we become
as we become who we are

the sun also shines
     on a shadow

and shadows cool
 even the warmth
  of the sun

fire has swum over the sea
    to burn in a darkened land
as the sea has doused
    the fire
the flames you hold in your hand

   the brushing of leaves on trees
these are the sounds that come rushing
    to my ears as i sit in the burning
sun one with the shadowy leaves i hear rustling

la tabla rasa
i do not go along with that philosophical idea
but i do like the symbol of the tabla rasa
the blank slate
it is what we all look for
search for
when i write this screen is blank
i scroll up
i think is the word
so that there is nothing but blank slate
i do not like having the words
affect me
i want to start afresh
that is pure
at least to me

i just did it again
now only these two lines appear in front of me
i will wipe away all three and write a poem

i am a peaceful man but no saint
if a mosquito bites me
whether it is instinct
or un momentito de anger
i try to stop it from biting me
am i trying to kill it?
what does it take to get a mosquito
to stop biting?
in a millisecond i

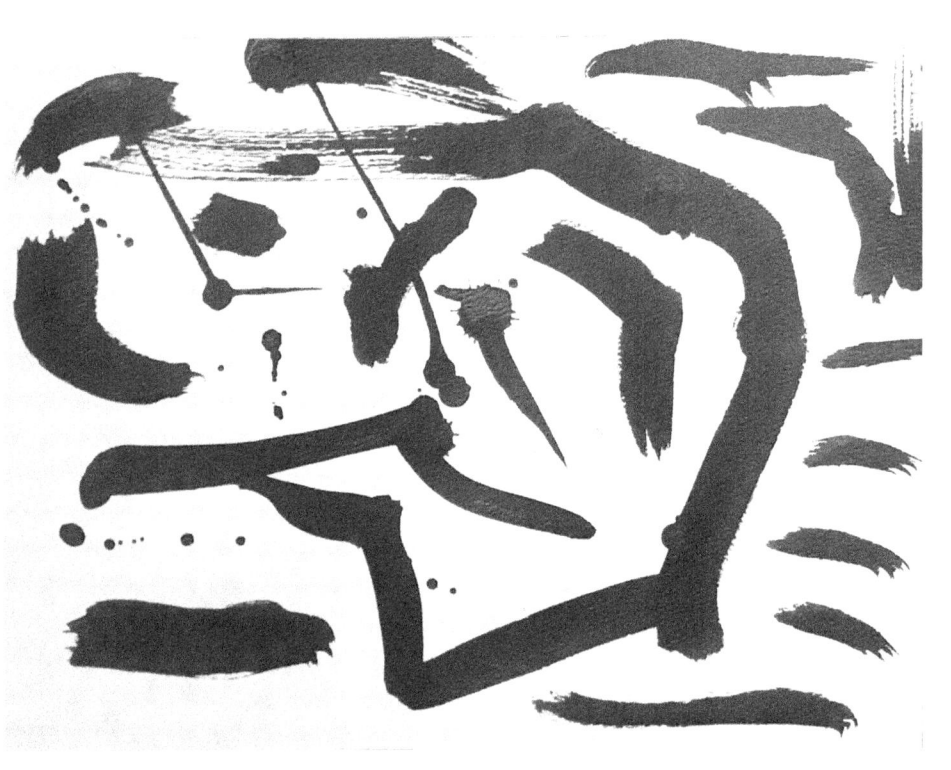

oh great wise one

where are your six strings
      one i see hold up your pants
           (i understand we must cover our nakedness)
then where are your five strings
      i see one you have tied to your pet
           (or perhaps a companion)
well then where are your four strings
      i see one is tied to your hair
           (so full and soft)
then where are your three strings
      one i see tied around your money
           (so much)
well where are your two strings
      i see one tied you to your wasted existence
           (oh too short)
well then where is your one string
           (come on tell me)
      do not be tongue tied

you must speak the language of the audience
almost like a translation at first allow the
people to come with you on a mini tour of the
musical education
show us how little we know can mesh into the
beauty that is the artist
the writer   the painter   the dancer
show us that you are one of us
do not for a moment put yourself above us
with your education or any other mystical gifts
that you might have
not for one moment
can you think to be better than the people that
are working and slaving away in these factorys
that do nothing but continue the people forced
to slave away in the mines that do nothing but
support the degradation of not just the earth
itself but the people of earth forced to work in
these places
get an education
it is there lot in life
i can not support the whole earth
they seem happy
heres a little something for the lady
she costs $100
a guess its not a necklace
or a wedding ring

same thing
i here the telephones ring
dingaling ring a ding ding
the most beautiful woman in the world is
no more than a woman
and the ugliest woman in the world is
no less than a woman
it is just whether or not your version
your personal belief of what
in fact
a woman is
what her role is
what her destiny fate a future holds
do you think that women are like animals
to be hunted and pierced with your arrow
does it matter if they agree
if they agree then it is real
but if they do not agree
if they are convinced
sold
helpless
intimidated by your authority
or even your
majority
lets ask ourselves
"ask thine own soul to who
    thou not is true
        truly"

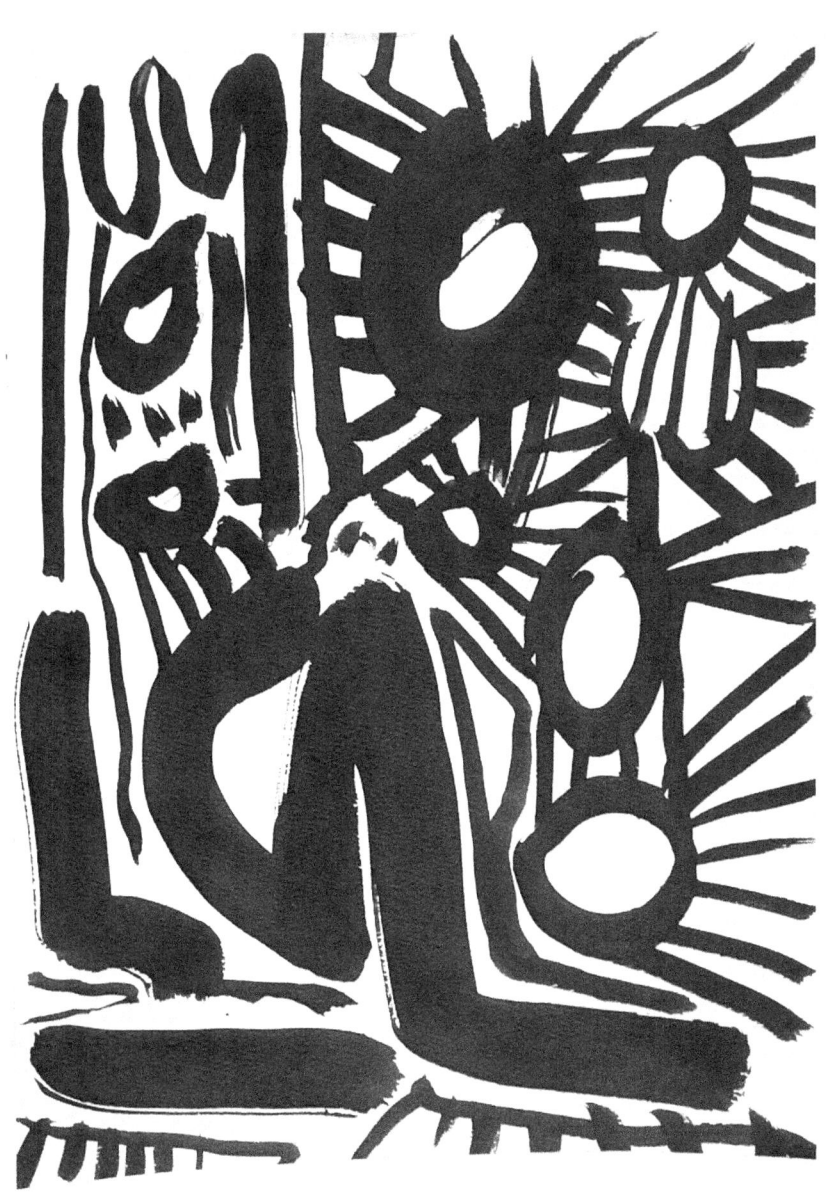

go where it leads
let it take you
it will take over your soul and
leave your spirit
out of control

i dreamt of two indians
american
native american
first nation
from the land that we call the americas
we were talking about population
and the population before the white man came
how the white man said that there was
nothing here
so they built something
that is total bullshit
and they still say it
this land
like china
like africa
like south america
like ireland
like vietnam
was militarily conquered
and then culturally enslaved
pioneers
pilgrims
explorers
colonists
conquistadors
trappers

soldiers
observers of the native people
all these people are the same person
an outsider
a foreigner
gringo
turista
extranjero
étranger
colonist
lookin at the natives like a zoo exhibit
when really they are just trespassing in
someone elses land
living on borrowed time
and stolen fruit
tainted water
a temporary respite
from the pain of reality
and time

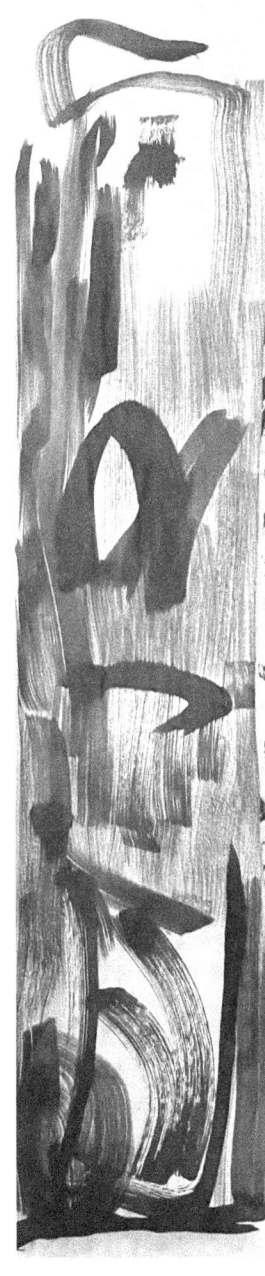

i feel the verse flow within me
     perhaps it is the cuban beat
       beating an endless
          rhythm
     of the imagination
  flowing from within to get out
  flowing from without to get in
     converging
      merging?
        drifting
        mixing
nix on the criminals around us
     are within but also
        without
          an ounce of soul
beyond control
        i will crawl into a hole
     in order to protect me from
        the bombs that only burn your
        soul
beyond control
        like a sabertoothed mastif
     tiptoeing through the moons

drowning in the waves of suited whores
    not mine and certainly not
                      yours
after the wars we all deserve a long rest
    in the grooving roll of a hickory grove
  a treasure trove
      that was stolen from above
built with love
    in the name of love
        on the grave of true love
          never found again
        the true one
        known
           a moment
             too
        much like the moment you are
        living
            in this moment
   a moment of clarity
        the search goes on
            was that it?
as slowly creeping to arrive
      silence returns
               to drown out
      the whispered screams
           of her farewell
        farewell
      her screams
       whispered

in a moment drown by a silence
previously unknown
silence returns
to drown out

the whispered screams of her farewell
rush by
i watch her go
two black silken legs   rush by
i watch her go
paralyzed in the mist of her midst
i worship from afar
because i am
so far
away
perhaps another day will flow
into the rippled eddy
flowing from rock to bank
and around again
on to further shores
watching
as the water passes
the cascade
weeps
in
its
un
moving solitude
to await

                another moonless night
                        the ongoing search
                                for the
                                land of your birth
                from where did the spirit come
                 from where did this arrive
                        in the life of another
                                one like you
                 alone there waiting for
        a moment of clarity
                        as you sit ask yourself
                                was that it?
or was that just the day rolling
                                ever flowing
                the shimmering weaves of
the winds waves
                        caressing the long grass
                climbing
                        twisting turning
                  up the rolling hills
                        pristine in their
                                observation
                        of the vampid coast
         a flash
                        in the back of an extinct
                                form of transport
                        not suitable for the whims of man
                                let alone the whims of
                        the everpowerful

     spirit breathing
    a soft caressing
      breathe
    along the long grass
     golden jade
     glittering
   in the suns unseeable glow
   true as one blade of grass
explaining everything
as i go along
but who wants to be bored with stupid
overthinking
analyzers
feel the voices around you and write what the
music tells you to write

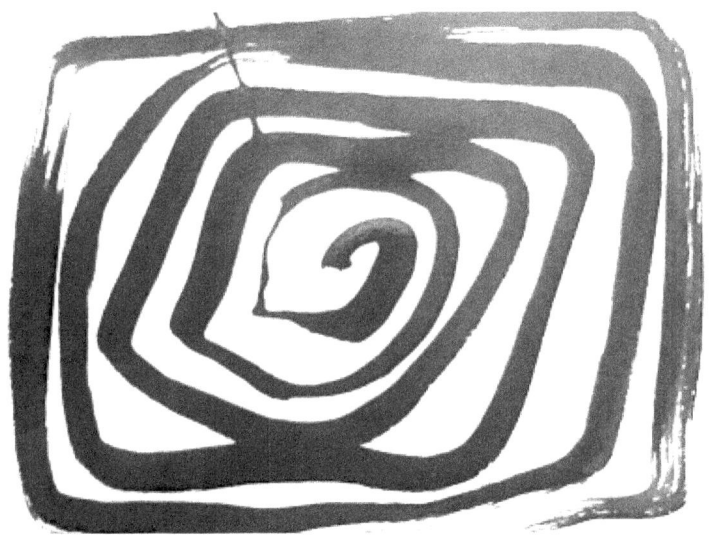

the months disappear like a veil revealing the
truth
a veil
easy to hide behind
by choice or out of fear
we all wear a veil
many faceted
many hued
changing with the reason in the mind
i am trying to learn how to live
without the veil
without the different shields
without the different protective devices

now as then
the people move
and flee
and fear
and fight
always running from the men of might
warriors not poets
killers not of the song
an uncertain mixture within all of us
some well saturated
or well seasoned
by the land
can by great
well seasoned
by the land
is power

forced to leave
thus forced to think
and dream
of the beauty of home

destined to wander
in wonder
till the moment
when we can all
return
to a homeland
so far away
but there
the land of my soul
the place of my heart

unknown inspiration had come from the disappearance of shadow. a letter a postcard note who knew. but in my hands the words now flew. from where they were to where i sat. i read from my fingertips. shaking my head at symbols to me not known. but beautiful. visions. and visuals from afar. outside of the city. away from this existence that so many of us commit to. why. the options takin away in the buzz of times alarm. for how can an unknown option be chosen. it was in this world that i read

a stolen sun
a coast dreamt outside of time
breaking waves woven in the wash of the mind
who wrote this
who saw it
who felt it
who shared it with me
paradise arriving in the shadow city
the automobile the rolling waves
the streets of petroleum smothering the natural
path within the trees
buildings blocking the swaying breeze
no longer caressing the palms bending with
ease

could this world truly exist or is this only a dream
a vision of another time
but no place now
nonexistent in this concrete forest the rock carved into blocks and cells. molded for the strength of a thousand reeds. to conquer the nature that even here in the city will not be conquered.

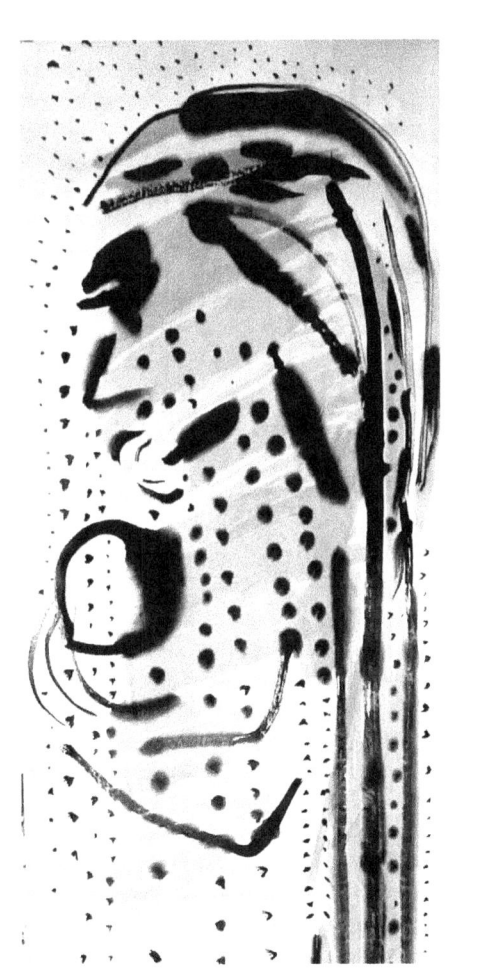

paralyzing fear as a kid. was i the only one that knew? different from the others. did my silence radiate an inner calm? that calm ever present on my shell. perhaps i am the prophet of happiness. i am happy. but why the fear? of pain and bitter loneliness. my idea of happiness is so foreign. even to me.

the water flows in streams
the fruit from trees does grow
you are a fool if you dont listen
i am a fool
because i know

who is the fool
a cowards words unsigned un claimed. a human can not live if the human is yet unnamed. a fool tries to live life as a dream. look around you. this is not a dream this is reality. the reality not a reality. do you think i need your words to remind of this hell i live. the noises crawling from the window into my mind. blinding the music that sings within us all. no there is no music. the radio is silent. i sing and they tell me to shut up. there is no music for the poet is dead. perhaps his words washed up on the shores of a sunken island. to bob in the tides of useless time.
who is the fool

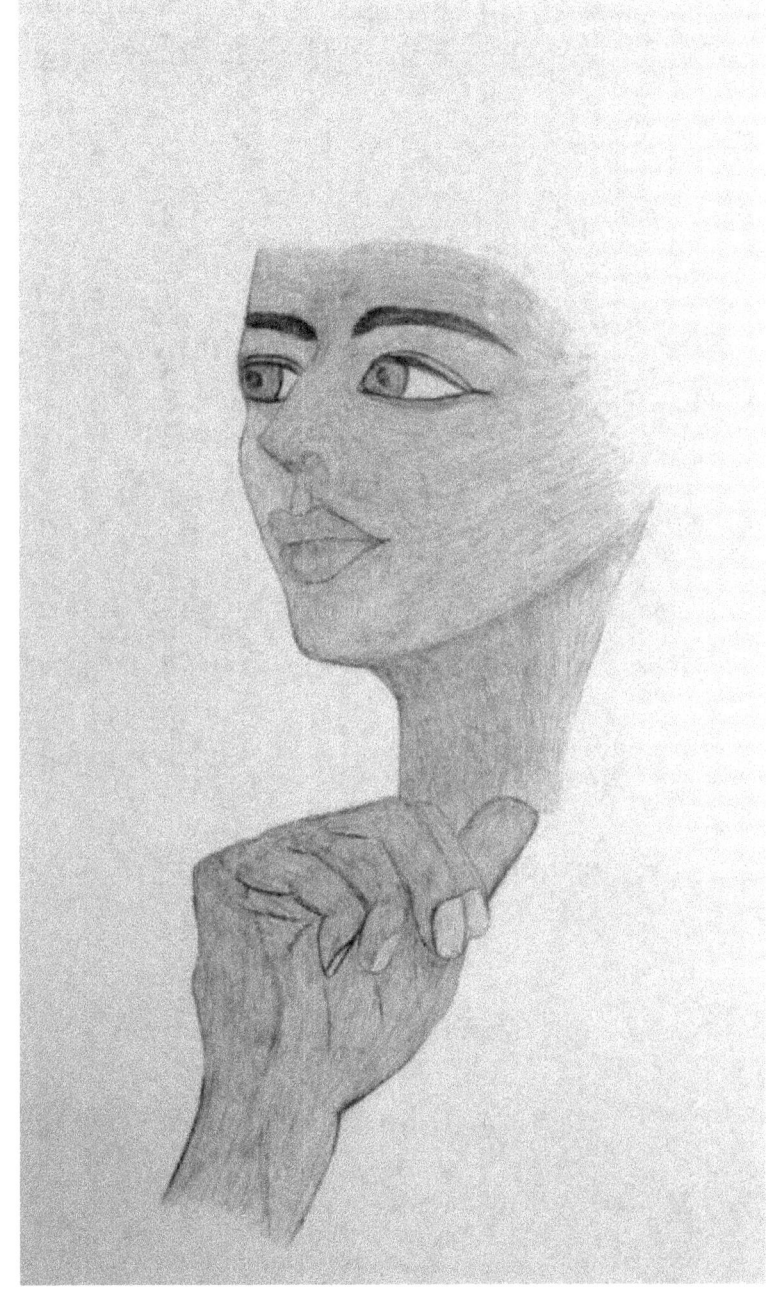

the rippled eddy swirls
flowing from rock to bank
and around again
watching as the water passes
the cascade weeps
in its unmoving solitude

the swirl of the water
flowing collecting
the drops of the avenues
spinning along the road
watching as the water passes
and falls through his arms
the drain weeps for its
momentary
embrace
now dry
and empty
only a steel drain
in the embrace of petroleum
street

i promise to stop searching
if you promise to be true . . . .
silence

i promise to stop searching
let me feel to know . . . .

i promise to stop searching
i will sit and wait
i will live
i will enjoy every moment
just tell me that that is the right thing
that that is truth
that that is true knowledge
that that is understanding . . . .
nothing.
only a breeze softly brushing against my cheek

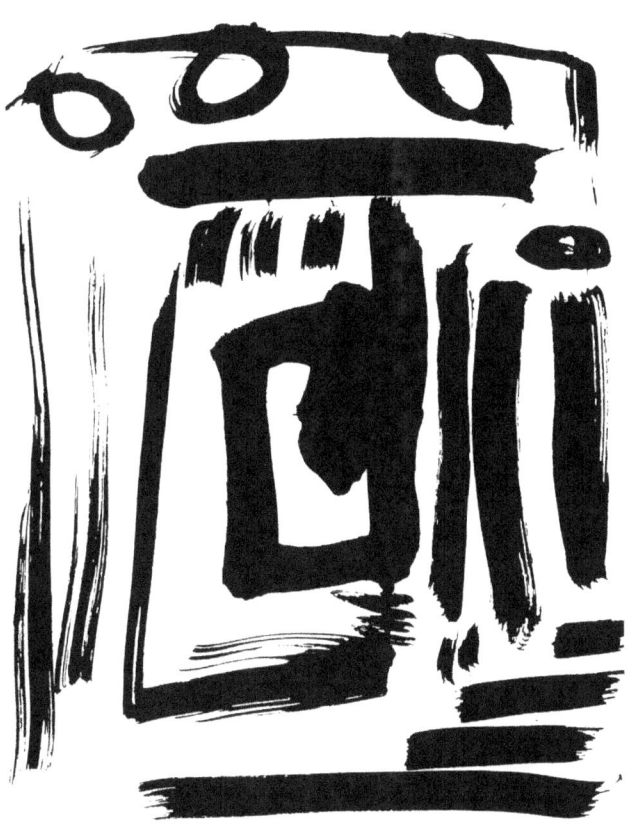

i am surrounded by thousands of my brothers.
sisters. fathers children friends. i walk down the
street. look up to say hello. they stare only at
their feet and without a word they are gone.
why do we feel that we need to be alone. why
do we not look up and smile. solitude is
empowering but the company of our fellow
humans is what makes us humane. perhaps that
is just the point. the bandit of loneliness does
not only attack when you are alone.
always the bandit is lurking
poised
for attack

sweeping through the grass
stepping strongly
in the dew
still wet from the half moon spray
i push the dog away
torn between the worlds of the still
and shaking branches
i fall into the swirl
of the lush
embracing
leaves

awoke true to himself
how hard it must have been to be truly who he was
the woman said it and she is right
everyday we must be true
so hard in this world created in the mind of another
anothers loves
anothers ways
anothers world
our own within
and so often we are without

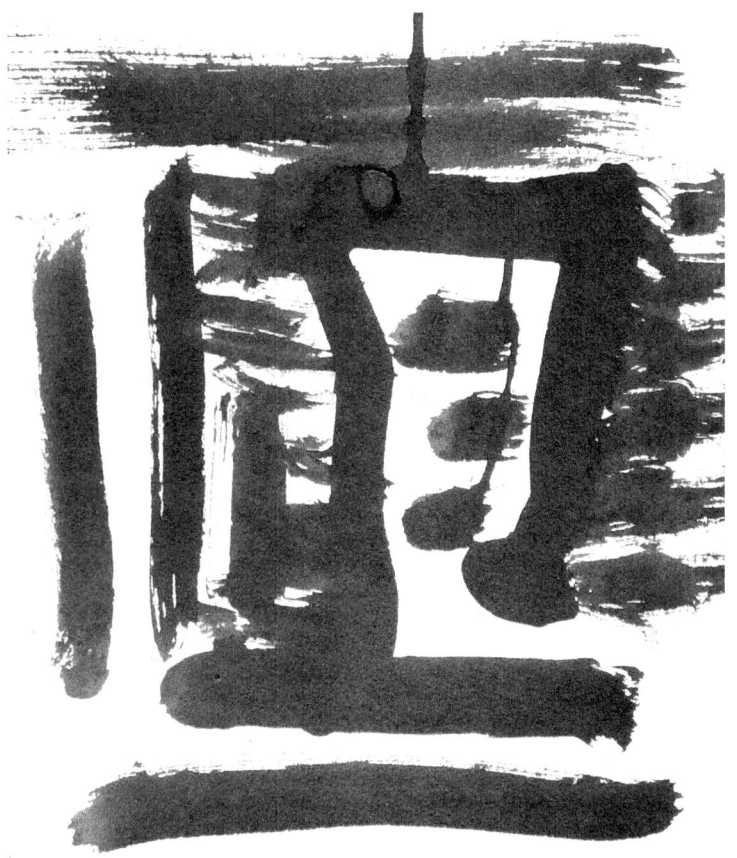

never before has so much been seen as what it truly is not
in the blink of an eye the shapechanger is trapped frozen in the ice of a cold heart
from the start the truth is the true medicine
life being the form of inception?

freedom is not a gift to be
          taken away for
            inappropriate? behavior
freedom is life
and life means freedom
which in its essence is
                    untouchable
                    ungraspable
                    unbreakable
                  unknown
  but cherished in the flash of its goodbye
that any man can judge me
that any man can punish another
that any man can be judge
entonces ye will be judged
i powerless sit in their cell
a day in the arms of your justice
curing disease
        the disease those that will not be enslaved
by your laws of paper

backed by the violence of the true weapon
the money to buy a title
or a gun
or a car
or authority
sanctioned only in the halls of your walls and cells
as if four walls could enslave a soul
nor cold steel bars imprison the mind
the wings of humanity
                    are within
     and always
            the eagle will soar

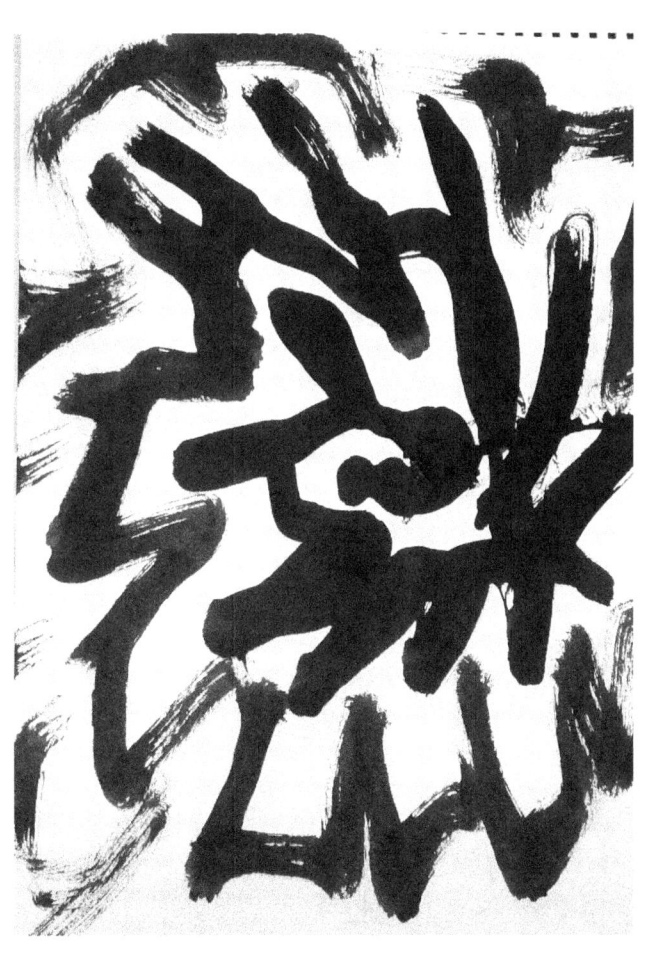

words need be said
or the soft soul will die
words must be read
for the soul to stay alive

THIS WOULD BE MADE UNIVERSAL
(((((You are human)))))
you are an artist now just go for what you have to do
you know that what you are doing is correct
you no that you have to do that which you are doing
you have no choice
you are what and who you have always been
never be ashamed
never hide who you are
just be you
and know that within you are you

and the outside is just the meat for what is inside
cleanse the inside
ease the inside and live the proper life
you are a good person
allow yourself to be a good person
be nice
be happy
and try to be nice to everyone
pet all the dogs
pet the cat
smile
look into the eyes
stop and chat
there is all the time in the world

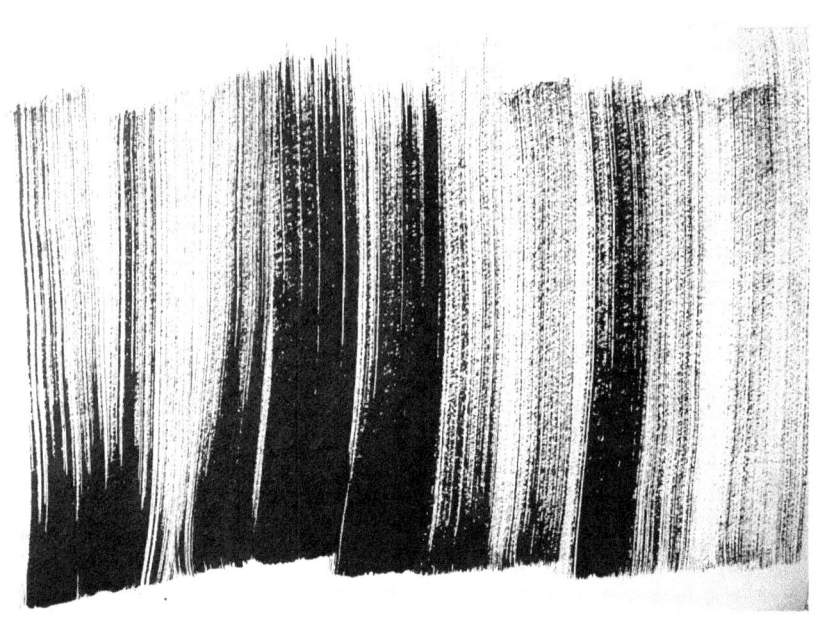

my hands shake when i do not write
my mind aches
my back aches when i write
my mind wakes

my soul sleeps when i do not think
my hands cry out for a warmth
my heart bleeds when i write
my strength flows in ink

always i think of the words
often times i write them
always i think in words
sometimes i agree

i finished my burger with fries and a guinness
a piece of pie
i relaxed and thought about the moment
suspended in time
ad infinitum (forever permanently)
the day is beautiful
the trees stand tall
black squirrels scramble
along the lush grass
glistening in the evenings
   spring
along the river the mallards
   call a song of
         coming night
ducks and babys
   wade towards home
 cascade a humorous bridge
    rocks and slabs tickle the flow
water swirls
   unstoppable
       a lone leaf
         of a maple tree
hovers above the waters surface
   levitating on the flow of days
            and nights
        and again
     peaks through the sun
    to spill day

these boots
so strong
but my feet
in them
so weak
and all that strength is for nothing

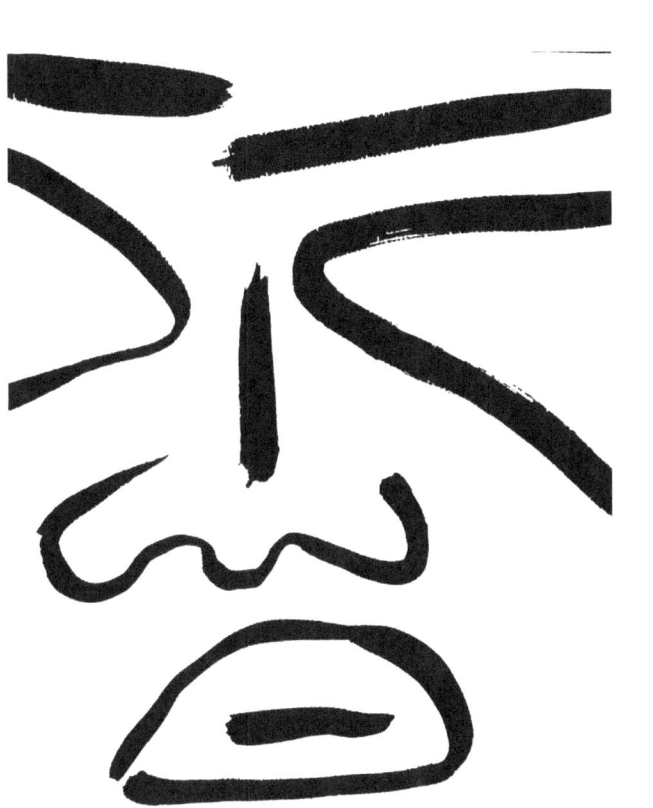

the cars never seem to slow. cruisin. passing in a steady mountain stream. the mist rises and is not the mountain spray. black petroleum river. canoes of steel. sitting in a dug out machine. inside the machine. i am better off . sitting here . smoking a cigarette . sipping a xokolatl. con crema. at least trying to relax and enjoy. life is the greatest gift. the sun peaks from behind the receding morning dew. her heat collecting and conquering. as the sun always will. shadows crawl across the branches of the trees. receding to siesta for the high hours. the sun high. in the sky that is clear turquoise swirling above the shimmering desert hills. a suharo stands tall. a scarecrow in the field of sand. protecting the magic seed of the fertile field. not seen in the blindness that comes with sight. and lack of vision. a sip of the xoko. not quite hot enough. i guess when you move so slow. i would say i move at a different speed than the other kids. slower. but speed is really not a factor in this life. they can convince you that it is. but they would be lying. they do not know thus could never say and to see is merely to illuminate the fact of their very ignorance. a fact that perches precariously in the bow of a suharo. untouchable. known. seen but not heard like the best tykes. go far away with your shining bikes. needle poke. and nails are drilled in the bit that is said and a moment of talk. seen before. not so fast. total momentary existence to be constantly present is more than to say i am in the present it is to feel the present in every cell every molecule of your body. i am alive. that is my proof not the words but the awareness of each and every momentito. cada. todos los. qualquier momento. that is what a candorous person would say. i guess that tells you a little bit about the other kids. right hand reaches to sip koko. crema at the top of my lips. the sun shaded my shades. the word for the glass that shades the eyes from the sun. shaded.

a note on the counter
--> please take out
recycling
for your
more than understanding
current roommates

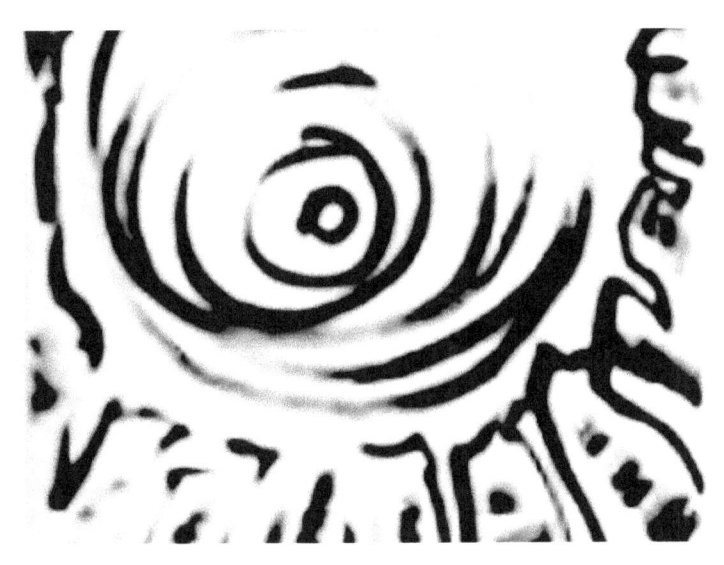

i realize
now
what i have been searching
for
for so long
i realize
now
that
what i have been searching
for
for so long
is a nameless symbolless
lightless
darkless
foto
perhaps it is a photo
from when you were
a child
or a photo from the first time
you
knew what love is
or the first time
you realized how beautiful
the pine trees
are painted
when the sun sets in the evening
shadows standing tall
in the eye of an all powerful storm
perhaps it is a photo

of someone you love
a mother
or a father
a sister
a brother
a friend
and the look in their eye when you know that
you are together again
perhaps it is a photo
of someone who died long ago
living on in the image of your
mind
can you hear the words
they speak
do they speak softly
the look in their eyes when you know that you
are together again
or perhaps it is a photo
of a feeling
you felt
when you were a child
and all the important people
in your life
told you to
shut up
wakeup
stop it
be realistic
you did feel it

you did dream it
you did sing it
and you can
you will sing it again
as soon as you
realize
now
that what you have been searching
for
for so long
without a name
without a symbol
with neither light nor dark
is the look in your eyes
when you know
that you are together again

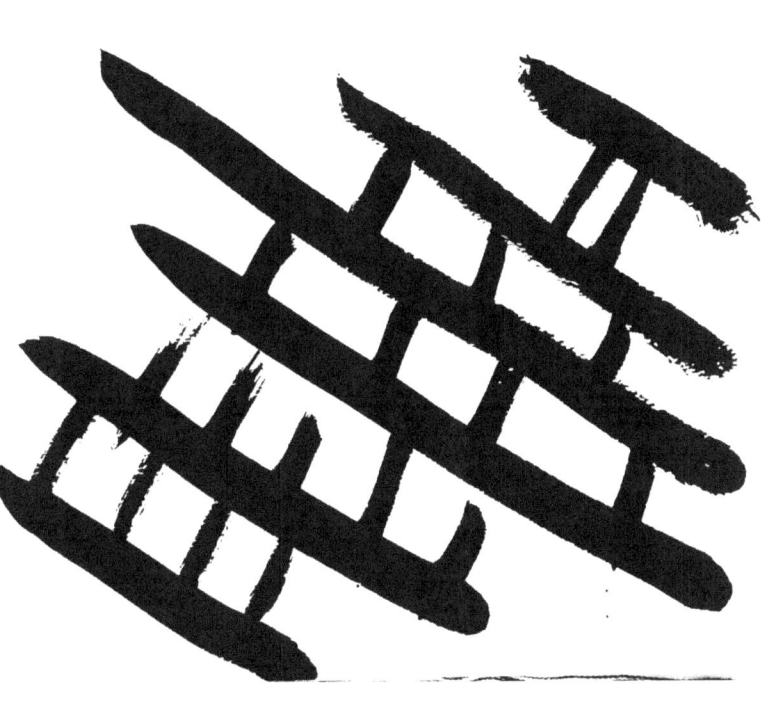

is it strange that i write every day
i do not think so
i breathe
even when i am sleeping
but i do not question why i breath
or if i am doing the right thing

sometimes when i write i write nothing
but that is the point
no thing can be nothing

it is the worshipped that worship
it is those that look up that are justified in looking down
and those that envy that are justified in their selfishness
they are on guard because they would think first attack
they protect what is theirs because they felt justified in stealing it in the first place
they are taught to worship their superiors thus taught to be superior
they are taught to do what they are told thus when they speak they expect the weak to do what they are told
they are taught that revolution will not be tolerated
thus they crush revolution
dissent is a sin and they condemn the heretic
the truth is a tool thus they wield the tool like a weapon

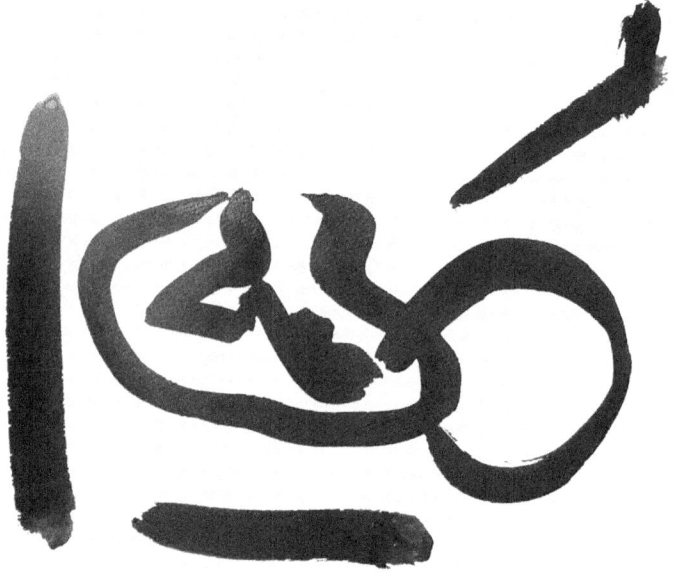

thou knowest not what thou has spawned
but the truly strong relax and yawn
let weeds grow on the lawn
drink and smoke til dawn
or
sleeping never see the dawn

do you know thou art a pawn
i awake in a dream and you are all gone
the greatest gift is life
and when that gift is loved above all else
wealth is known in the smile of all
the smile of a child
the smile of a friend
the smile of a mother
the smile of a lover

the us restaurant at green and stockton has closed
down the block a shoe boutique opened
shoes selling better than food these days

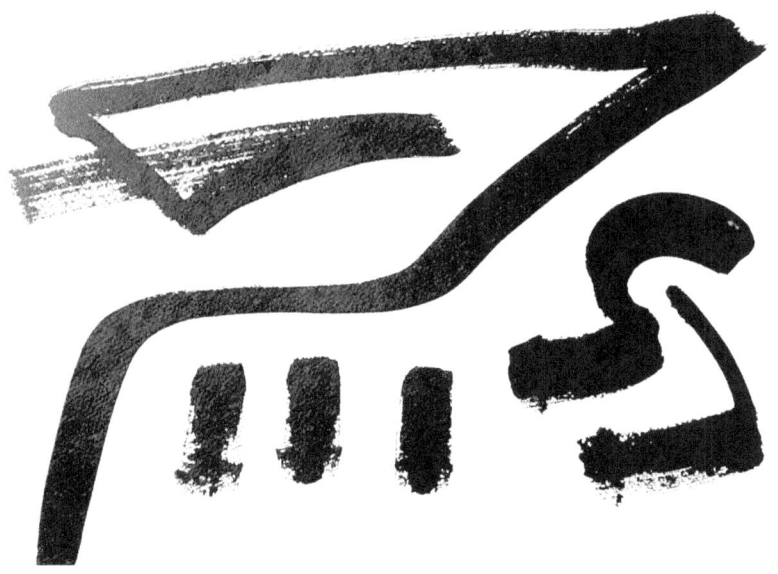

i was thinking of opening up an air boutique
that will sell you
air
but the air is free
see what i mean

wisdom of the ages
enter me
spirit of the ages
flow within me
love of the ages
love all

wisdom of youth
enter me
spirit of youth
flow within me
love of youth
love all

wisdom of the land
enter me
spirit of the land
flow within me
love of the land
love all

an old man sits on a couch
leaning to a table to type on a machine
skwinting up at the screen that is slowly taking
his sight
no one bothers him
no one calls

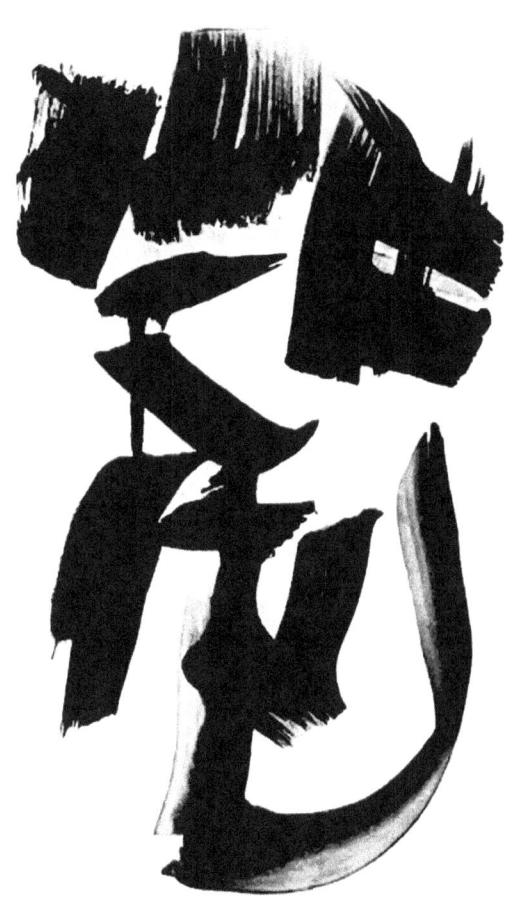

longing for something i will never have, to have it come so close, so near, to see it entering my grasp and then pulled away with a word. if only i had not felt what i knew i felt, it would be easy, if only i did not feel anything, but i do, if only i could not see that which is right in front of my face. if only my dream would cloud my vision and make me immune to that which is so near, and painful. a dream is in the distance, a true dream should stay there, every moment getting nearer, working, striving to achieve the dream, when the dream is so close, so real, suddenly it is not a dream anymore. it is truth, and truth can lie. without a word, without a sound the dream is seen for what it is and unless the dream stays far ahead it will not be what it was dreamed to be. to continue fighting, inch by inch, to continue working, line by line, that is what a dream is. and that is where the dream will stay. in my mind, i will continue to dream, to see, to grow,
because reality sucks. it hurts, and it can break your heart.

The curtain flies in the whistling wind, licking the off white wall, caressing the room brightened by the unusually clear sun, illuminating loneliness, slapping the silent in the face, for they have stuttered, not tempting, afraid of thinking it could be better, love is real, but not until it is known. how can we know love until we have known true love, allowing ourselves true love can only happen by leaving, forgetting and never going back to false or unsatisfying substitutes.

My heart is scar tissue. snap. cause she used it as a punching bag. snap. . snap. . snap but not one of those big ones, one of those little speed bags snapsnapsnapsnap.

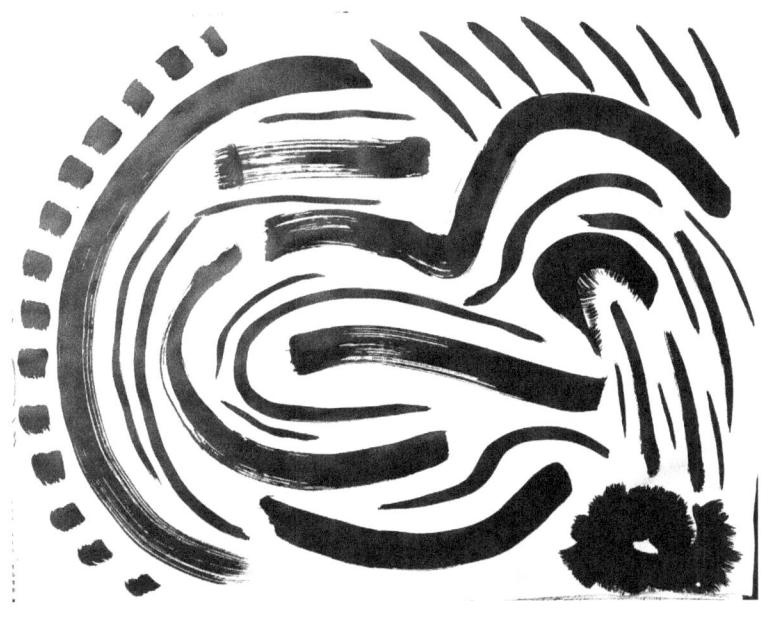

The Rain Pours Down
Splattering the pavement. Shattering the silence. Thunder clapping. Lightning flashing. Years since this. the summer rains. Riding in the puddles on the driveway. Drenched. the water soothing.
washing everything - away. renewing. Knowing. cooling.
Mist enters through the open door. A hammer slams. A flash jumps across the sky. illuminating. grab me. I run out into the Falling Spray. immersed in the joy of a time gone bye. Right Now. The trees and brush flash recognition in the shadows of the hazy distance. water.
I listen. steady. plodding. settled in. A pounding recurs. the sky ignites. a strengthening of force focusing the pressure. constant, drumming on the tile. the backbeat of nature. bass of thunder. clattering fleeting lead flash of the lightning. continual rhythm. Gone. washing down the stone streets. carrying the earth with it as it flows to the ocean.
Completing the cycle. pouring through existence, the sky becomes the screen. A

momentary daylight. A tropical flash from memory. as we all flow back to the source. Completing the cycle. beating through existence, the sky becomes the scream. A momentary fright. A tropical crash of memory. we go back. forward. the beauty. to rinse away - a river of pain - slips away. washing over me as i lay in the green grass. immersed in my own solitary flow. a cricket sings - beckoning the end. the energy retreats. victorious? accept the pain. gone now. beaten. bright. washed away. Completing the cycle. beaten through survival. the entire being becomes the dream. A momentary delight. A tropical dash of memory. as we all flow back on course.
Completing the cycle.

Always in my thoughts, always in my dreams. a dream of love, a dream of happiness, a dream of a life from dawn to dawn and moon to moon. filling my mind, filling my soul. conquering my heart. always. with me. always around me. always in my thoughts. always in my dreams. Perhaps someday in my arms.

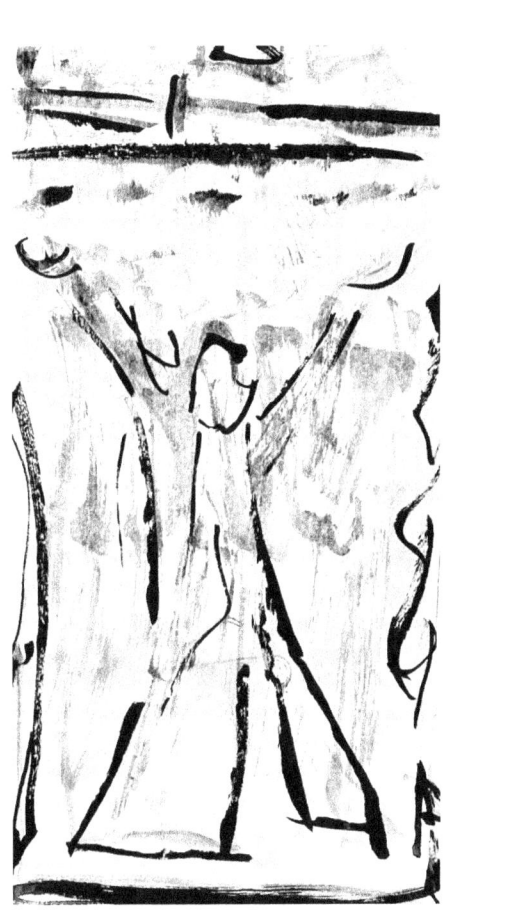

I KNOW NOTHING

all i know is that i feel, i feel love for everything, not always expressed properly, i understand everything, not always properly explained. even to my self. i feel a one ness with all. a connection, momentarily swallowed up by a canyon of separation. dual. the dual. the duel of truth. the war that will be waged until the last ? breaths the air of ? or drinks the ? of ? who am i to say who is qualified to discuss truth, to comment, to question, to answer, to know. all i know is that i feel, love for everything, not always expressed, not always understood, i understand everything, not always expressed, not always understood, the signal from my truth to my conscious travels a bumpy road, pot holes, detours, roadblocks, construction sights, traffic jams, floods, frozen, melted, snowed in, washed out, turbulence, high pressure situations, low pressure zones, total consciousness, of the unconscious. how? effort or nothingness. find it or wait for it. seek it and miss. trip over it and know. fall into truth.

tumbling through understanding. sitting on a rock of knowledge, complaining cause it is a bit damp, walking with the beam of understanding but only seeing that it is dark, swimming with the floatation of knowing, forgetting that to sink is to journey, to journey to see, to see. truth. who am i to say what is seen and unseen. who am i to say what is known or unknown, all i know is that i feel, and love, and understand, what little i feel, and love, and understand.

laughing, singing, dancing. Opiates of the masses? i could not help but need more, are thinking, talking, screaming any different? the music is too god damn loud, all i can do is scream which is exactly what i am doing right now just sitting staring thinking at least trying to. silently. better to sneak up on them, if they knew what i was thinking they would lock me up, then what use would i be? none. what use am i now? about the same but at least i am free, in my head, when i am free of body then i will truly be free. i sipped my wine imagining contentment. a dirty word.
and anyway i had to get a piece of food out of my teeth.

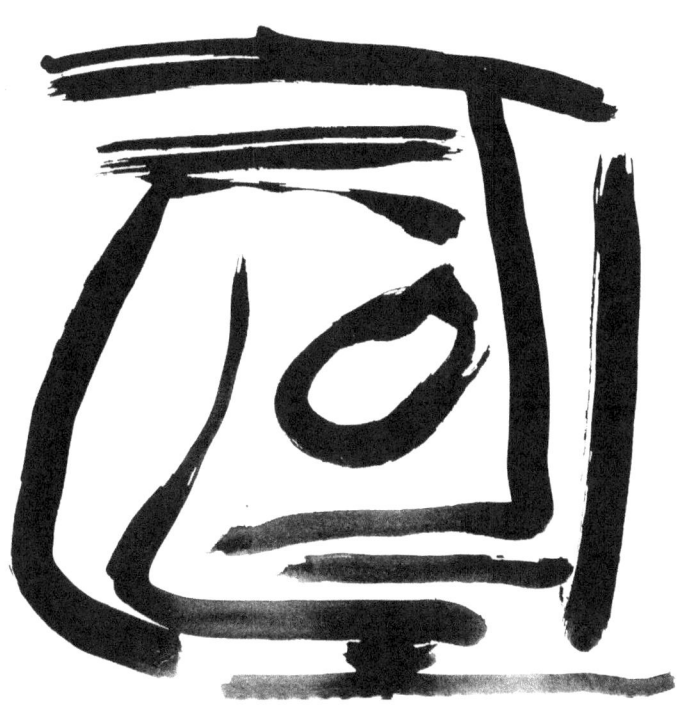

so yes some of these poems are bad, some are only good, while others possibly brilliant. but if we agree on the bad and find all the faults, or if we alight from the same as all the others, what matters. what is the difference. a word, a phrase, a line, an idea. endless possibilities. only open doors. none are closed. unless you close them, but burro meat is not transparent. and why try to keep out the light?

Everyday we live
looking seeking searching
hoping to reach
   what we are reaching for
that which we see is telling us listen.
  To be able to see is a gift, a burden, a weight.
it can paralyze, blind and crush the weak.
the strong of heart,
of soul,
will not be paralyzed
they will act,
they will not be blinded
they will see,
they will not be crushed
they will rise above.
But what good is it to rise above only to be alone.
to see is a gift,
to act a duty,
but true responsibility is not to the self,
it is to benefit those that can not or will not see.
Nishkama Karma, Selfless action.

i looked out the window at oblivion
but as i look closer
i realize
it was not oblivion after all.
it is the outside
trees
bushes
dirt
cement
concrete
the clouds
the sun
some people
a dog
a gas station
the grocery store
a cat jumps over the fence
must be tryin to get away from that dog.
i wonder where oblivion is

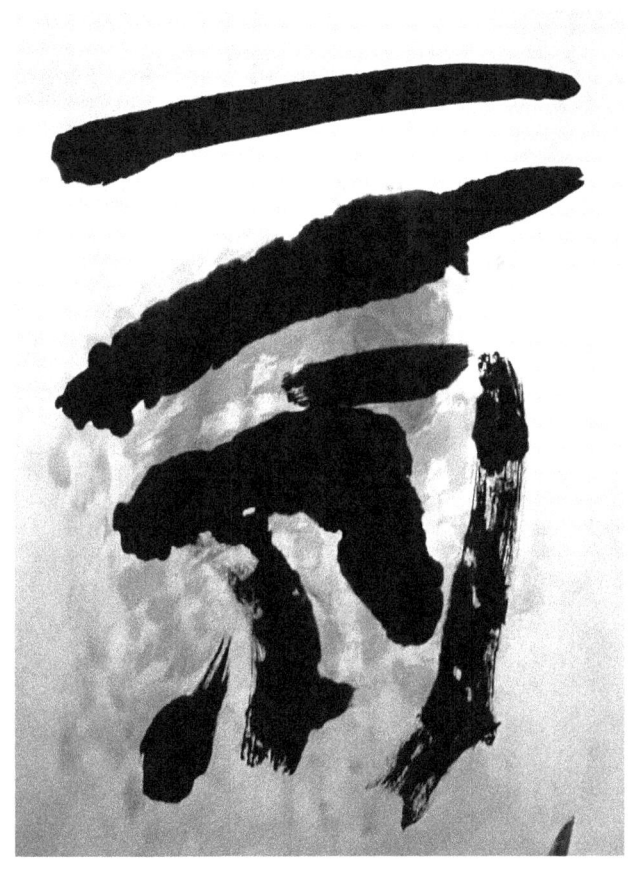

the warm liquid washes over my body, bathing
in sensation, light seeping into consciousness.
content, levitating above, I flow with the liquid,
one. all around, touching, feeling, knowing,
seeing for the first time or the last time.
i will never lose this feeling, complete comfort,
complete joy everything beauty warm soothing
i want to stay.
feeling please don't leave

i have broken the net. my soul has escaped. the rope of expectation
intertwined with thought. learned or nature. perhaps every learned thought pushes nature out of the road. my road was strong. malleable. it pressed close but stayed truth. crowded. often to overflowing. but it would not let nature seep away. lost forever. to the dreck shoveled in our heads the moment of our release from the pleasure of the womb.
the long journey back. momentary splendour. only to rise to the surface and realize that it is beautiful. but not home. rise to the surface to see only that which is physically around you. surrounding you. the easy focus. hiding without thought for the invisible. surrounding us. every inch. caressing. comforting. loving. if only we would stop. allow the pleasure to enter into our every pore. life. spirit. engulf me. i take you. consume your vital juices. your essence buttery on my flesh.
hold me.

i had been searching for forever
looking all around
i traveled to the deepest reaches
hoping for a sight
i sat to wait
to let it in
to see if it can know
stood again and kept the pace
going faster
up and down
i sat to rest on a rock
but it was damp so i kept searching

i promise to stop searching
if you promise to find me . . . .
no answer

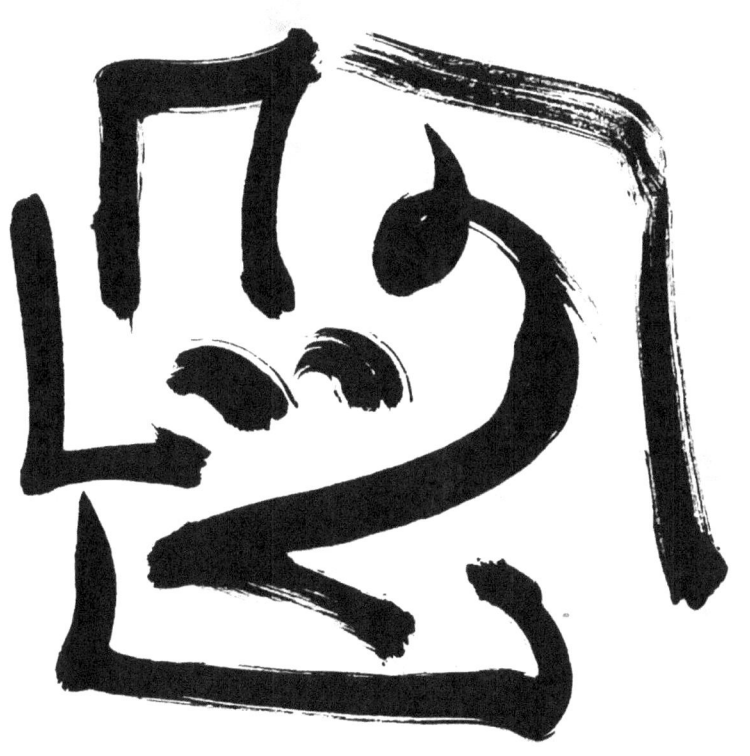

One day i will look up
perhaps already knowing
or one day i will turn
not understanding why i know
a feeling
a sense
deep
hidden
misunderstood
a number
i will look up
or turn
and our eyes will meet
after so long
after so much
before eternity
i will hold you in my arms and never let go
please do not make me

i do not want to gain at the expense of others
i only want to love
but it seems that i have to
to survive in this world
why is it like that?
why do we have to do this?
live like this?
why cant we just love?
Love.
i need you to tell me.
i need you to show yourself
i need you to appear again
i need you now. Now.

please tell me . . . . .
no answer.
it was so silent i could hear my heart beat

i have been sitting here waiting
i stopped searching
like i promised
i trusted you

i have not moved
i have done nothing
for fear i would miss something
but i am losing patience
i need you to help me
i need you with me
i need to know
i have not eaten in days
please let me see
let me know some way
i am sick of sitting here listening
to my stomach begging for food
give me comfort

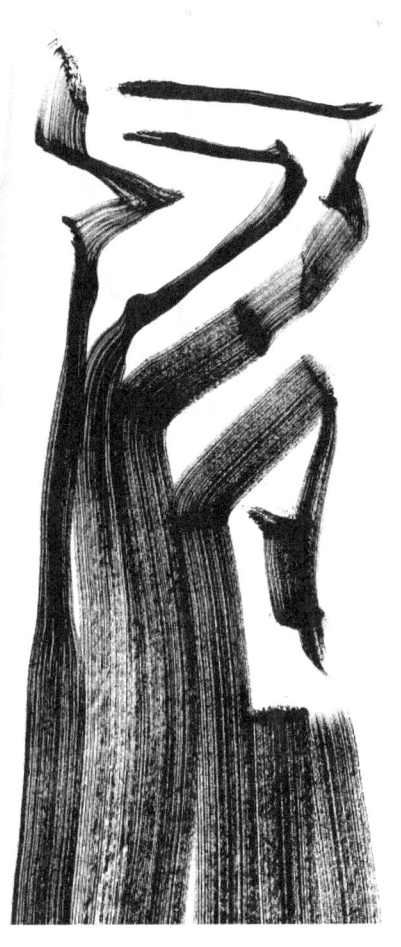

Down poor in soho
A downpour in soho
Drizzle
Sprinkle
Sideways glance
You lost the chance

Light showers
Purple flowers
It takes two to believe in romance
Dance
Pants
She wants
Without knowing
Thus loves without showing
Thus acts without thinking
Perhaps if i had been drinking
Woulda gone for it
Too mellow
Perceived as yellow.
So she attacked
Thinking that i lacked
The wherewithal to fight
Just cause i don't yell
If i truly want you to listen
I will cum close and i will

Silently scream
A whisper.
Sister
I am sorry that i missed her.
Certainly petty
Certainly pretty
Even for this city.
But that aint the point
I was enchanted by her
The very first time i met
Her

They told me
Do not look her in the eyes

some of these poems could suck. some might be brilliant. others a glimpse. this one disappointment. but those that are shit and those that glow with a luster saved for more colorful palates are often times mirrored. perhaps the same. the line between good and bad. the line between pleasure and pain. a holy man and a child. illumination and insanity.

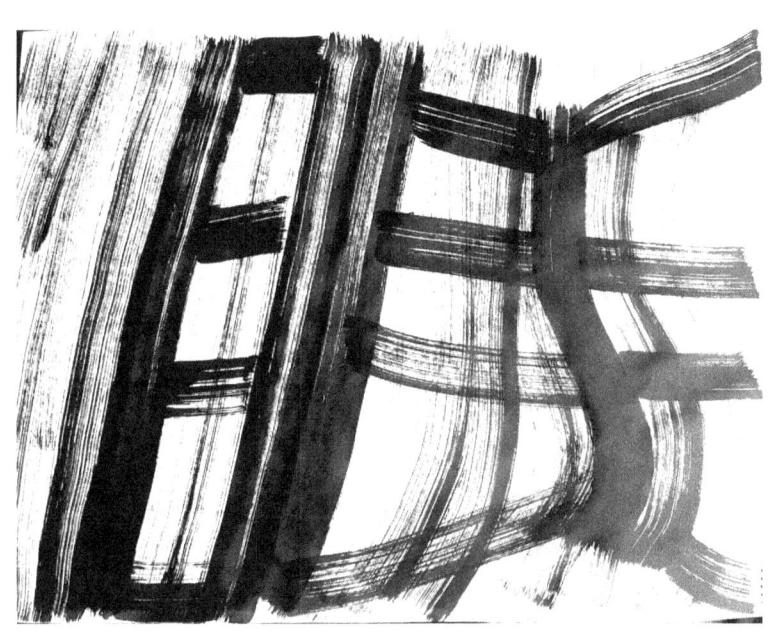

I close my eyes and the visual world disappears plunging ever further over come by my own darkness plug my ears killing all audible sensation hearing only the symphony of the mind stuff my nose halting sense of smell leave my mouth closed to dry and parch all senses off alone in my shell a temporary bodice conscious of being conscious of conscious i try to keep them off but they give me no choice the world is gone i can not see it or hear it or smell it and could never feel it, has it disappeared or is it there with or without me ever there for ever more ever spinning weaving the thread of life through time

cars. the automobile. driving down the road
fast
when you are walking
and you see a car
driving down the road
fast
watch   how fast they are going
then ask yourself
why?

the aggression they express while behind the
wheel. stays with them all day. everyday.
road rage. an animal trapped in a cage of his
making. speed his only expression of freedom
road rage. an animal trapped in a cage of her
making. speed her only expression of freedom.
            whats the difference

a new car every year. how can that not be
good?
i mean, if it is new
that means that it is improved
and if it is improved
that means that it is better
it seems like logic and reason to me
a boy medicated into submission
        dosed into a dream
        subdued by indoctrination

a poet an artist needs solitude
but along the cobbled stones of the road of solitude
lurks always
the bandit of loneliness

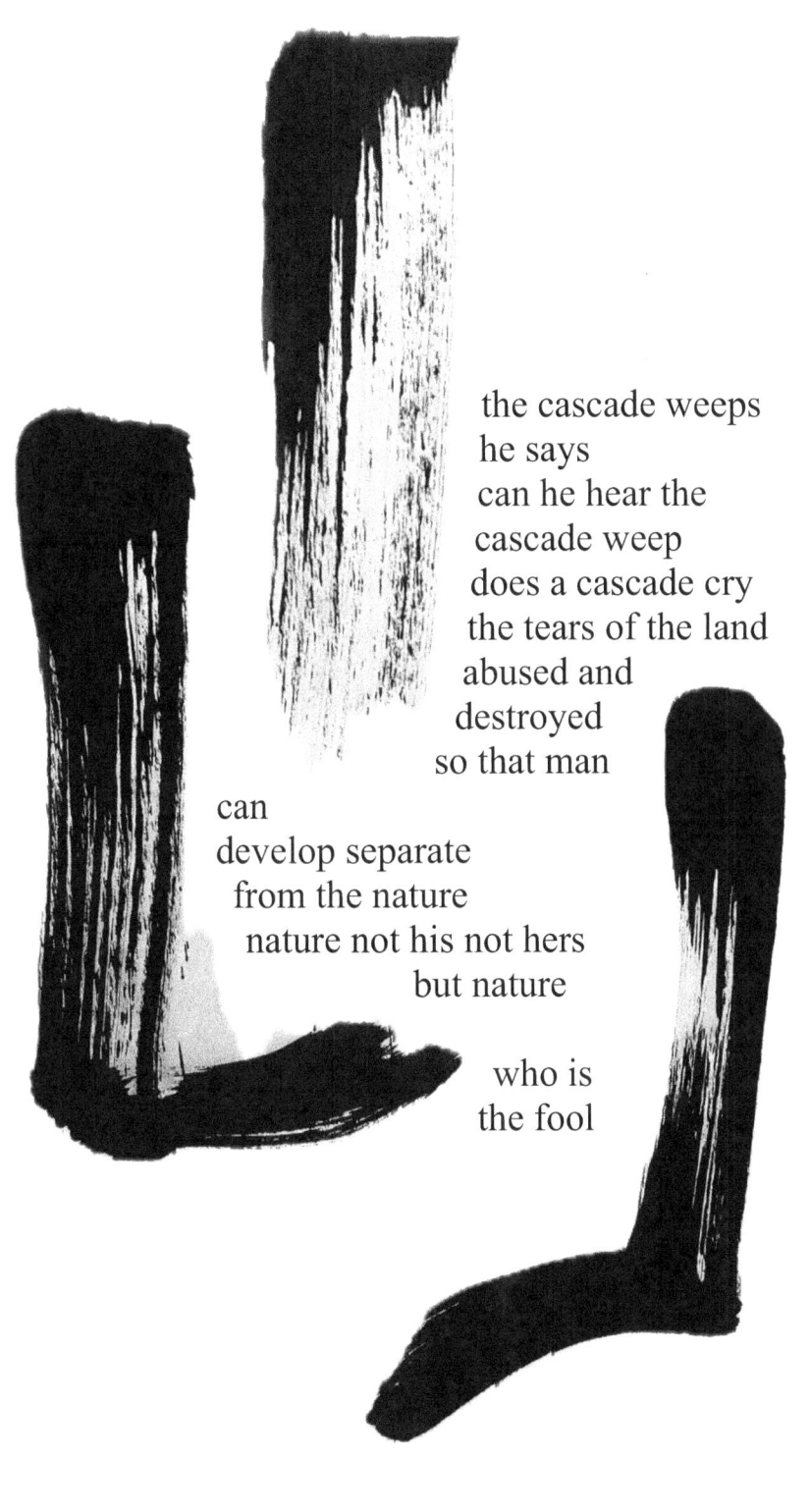

the cascade weeps
he says
can he hear the
cascade weep
does a cascade cry
the tears of the land
abused and
destroyed
so that man
can
develop separate
from the nature
nature not his not hers
but nature

who is
the fool

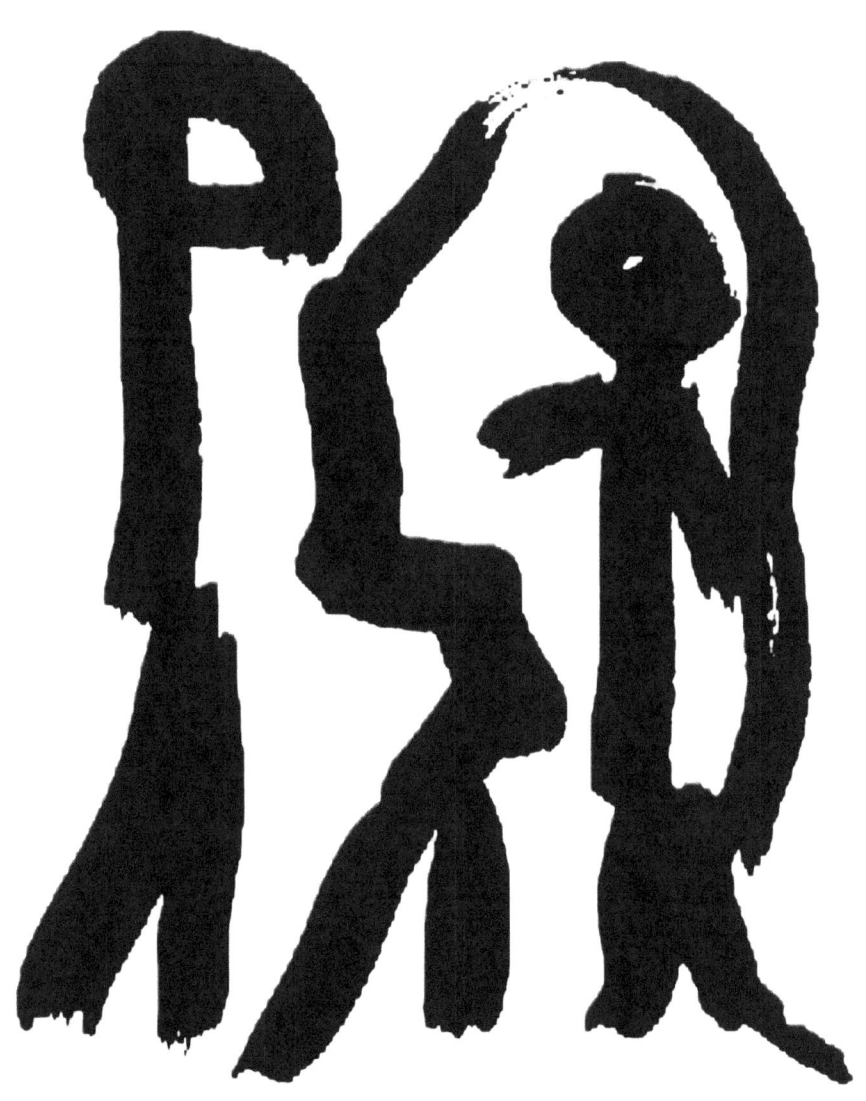

childrens story
shadow
green
forest

there was once a forest lush with the greenest
hues of all the earth
the sky would peer down through the clouds
and kiss the infant forest with the wind
cooling the warmth that the sun shone
the sun secretly loving the forest more than any
other piece of the earth.
and the sun was a hard one to please
but this forest was special
with trees short and tall
some wide trunked
some thin trunked
bushes and vines that caress and kiss the trees
flowers that seemed to bloom as if in thin air
roses as red as the evening sun says goodnight
lilys floating in the pools that become cool
clear crystal creeks streams and far away
occasionally to arrive with the wind from so far
away

the stream became a river and the river fell in cascades to quench the valleys thirst
great branches of color
so beautiful the name is merely beauty
petals of blue and yellow and red and purple and orange and all these colors when touched by the direct light of the sun would shimmer and shift to glow in colors represented by light alone
to be seen in silence
respected in the glare
petunias as pink as the cheeks of a caterpillar who it seems is inching along the large green leaves of one of the bushes and trees that feed him
that feed all the animals of the forest
that feed all the animals of the great valley
and that feed the wind and the air
cleansing and cooling the air when
our friend the air needed a bit of a shower
sometimes the air can not take care of itself but the trees and flowers understand and so they tell the air to cleanse itself
they allow the air to borrow all of the sweet smelling scents that when mixed create the aroma of beauty and freshness that makes all the animals that run around in the forest consistently more conscious

in fact if you go to the forest you will hear the
animals sing all the different songs
celebrating the beauty
and relishing the freedom that the forest
provides
with no strings attached
unless you count the vines
you can hear the birds high in the trees calling
far to each other
a squirrel scurrying up a tree
mouth full of nuts and more
close to the water listen for the toads and the
crickets
footsteps silently approaching perhaps a shy
doe
a deer
a female deer
spooked
watch her and her child run as to be flying
through the trees
soundless
and in the soundless moment from far away can
be heard the roar of what could only be a lion
the entire forest stops to hear the call
everyone likes to talk to the lion long distance
but few have the communicative skill to carry
on a conversation face to face
so they keep their distance
but not the invisible green jaguar

who looks through the trees and flowers and
branches and without a song and without words
communicates with the lion so far away
and in that moment slowly lopes behind a leaf
and is gone
to wonder what the green jaguar said with the
eyes
only
and as the birds relay the lions message a panic
spreads over the forest
the lion had seen that the animals of the
shadowy stone forest were traveling to the true
lush forest
it seemed that they were angry about something
and were going to steal the life from the forest
they wanted to steal the flowers and the trees
and the animals and the water
not realizing that the water they drank from the
valley was the same water that flowed within
these flowers and trees and bushes and lily pads
and animals and beauty
but the animals of the shadowy stone forest had
shown themselves over many generations to be
less intelligent than the animals of the lush
green forest
so lush and soft to the touch
and the animals of the lush green forest

after many years of trying to intermingle and mix with the animals of the shadowy stone forest
had learned only that the animals of the shadowy stone forest were dumb and mean and violent
never asking to borrow or share
never asking how they could have all that the animals of the lush forest
so green
have
of course the animals of the green lush forest
such fresh air
had talked amongst themselves
they had tryd at first friendlyness but with those animals of the shadowy stone forest it almost seemed like they did not know how to communicate
even amongst themselves
so now the lions warning had arrived
he being the strongest
not necessarily the fastest
but he was going to take a nap and the animals of the lush emerald forest
suggested he nap where he could observe the animals of the shadowy stone forest
where it seems a bit cold
certainly colder than here in the green forest so lush and full of life

trees and leaves that filter the sun and air
cleansing and freshening the air that all the animals needed
for this is the very essence of life
the animals of the shadowy stone forest
and the animals of the lush green forest
who knows how they filtered and cleansed and freshened the air in the shadowous stone forest
the only animals that went there from the green forest and never came back to this lush and beautiful forest were
a couple of birds
beautiful and very clever they used to mimic the other animals in the forest
they would keep us up night laughing with their dramas of the deer
and the beaver and the eagle
the eagle got a bit hot under the collar
but the one time that the show did not go over was when one of the beautifully colored birds started to do an impression of one of the animals
like always we had to guess
no one could guess and even the second beautifully colored bird could not guess
as we were thinking hard
the beautiful bird in the middle of his impression seemed to see a ghost over the heads of the audience

he turned green
and his eyes shined like jade encrusted
emeralds
a momentito
the jaguar the green jaguar
but as it was finally said the beautifully colored
bird flew as high as the highest branches
the second bird beautifully colored followed
we heard they tryd to check out the shadowous
stone forest
they never came back
we assume they either liked it or they are afraid
of the green jaguar
but i do not think they are afraid of the green
jaguar
the green jaguar does not speak much and
seems a bit different from the other animals but
the green jaguar has never been known to hurt
anybody
there is really no reason to be afraid of the
green jaguar

the animals that went to the stone castle and
never came back are prisoners
not all in cages
but the moat keeps the rats and mice and
rodents in
the parrots are in cages

a couple of snakes
dogs/coyotes/wolves
cats/cheetah
the green jaguar was crying because his baby was stolen
when he crys his emerald eye shine deeper than the sun and it blinds all those around the green jaguar
when he crys he can see through walls and trees and all and he saw the baby with the other animals in a stone and steel forest
lots of tall thin steel trees
that enclosed the different animals

now the animals of the stone forest are coming to the green lush beautiful forest
they are hunting all those things we said before
stealing trees to plant and cutting down other trees
diverting the water so that it goes into there moat
thus destroying the valley
taking the flowers so that they will die
trying to preserve them but not giving them any sunlight
because the stone forest is different than the green forest

and stealing the animals of the green forest for
pets and food
amusement for the perverted animals of the
stone forest

When we have time we will hear about how the different animals will do their part to free there brothers
helped by a few of the animals of the green forest
they invite the animals of the stone forest to live with them and a couple accept
Some day soon we will hear more about how shadowy the stone forest is
how pale and unhealthy all the animals of the stone forest are
how smelly the animals in their cages are
how dusty and messy the plants stolen from the green forest become when transported to the stone forest and how nice the couple that comes to the green forest with the animals of the green forest is

www.ingramcontent.com/pod-product-compliance
Lightning Source LLC
Chambersburg PA
CBHW052249220526
45471CB00001B/261